Memoirs of Suzie

71175-97

By
April Scales

All rights Reserved. No part of this book may be reproduced or transmitted in any form by any means, graphic, electronic or mechanical including photocopying, recording, taping or by any information storage or retrieval system without written permission from publisher.

The purpose of this book is to inform, educate and entertain. Although every precaution has been taken in preparation of this book, there may be errors or omissions. Neither is any liability assumed for damages resulting, directly or indirectly, from the use of this information contained within this book.

Published by:

SureShot Books Publishing LLC
P.O. Box 924
Nyack, New York 10960

www.sureshotbooks.com

Suzie is a fictitious name but the person is very real. The relationship that she has with her only child will bring a tear to your eye and a pain in your heart. Is this a good or a bad thing?

Acknowledgements

Thank you to everyone who made
this book a reality.

❧ About The Author ☙

April Scales is the author of "31 Days of Growth and Reflection."

When she is not writing, she spends time with her family and staying physically fit.

Chapter 1

In Sharon, Pennsylvania lived a young black couple by the name of Lillie and Aaron Barber. Aaron worked with steel erecting bridges. Lillie was a homemaker. They longed for a child but Lillie was barren due to a hysterectomy that she had at age nineteen. They decided that adoption would be the best option and visited the local foster care center.

A beautiful mocha-colored baby girl caught their eye. The baby had been abandoned at three months and was nameless. For paperwork purposes she was known as "Suzie." Suzie was plagued with asthma at birth and needed special care, aside from that she was healthy.

The Barbers took their bundle of joy home as a welcomed addition to their family. Lillie did not like the name Suzie so she changed it to Sheila Denise. The Barbers remained in Pennsylvania until Sheila was thirteen years old. The Barbers relocated to North Carolina in a small, rustic area near Family.

Chapter 2

Aaron gained employment as a night watchman and Lillie became a housekeeper for a very prominent white doctor and his family.

Sheila was nicknamed Gypsy by Aaron due to her carefree spirit. She was the type to never meet a stranger and enjoyed being the center of attention.

Sheila was a normal child who excelled in school and as she got older enjoyed her male peers. On an outing to the park she met the lifeguard who was a fair-skinned Cherokee boy with dazzling hazel-green eyes.

It was almost Sheila's sixteenth birthday and she had planned a party with a few friends that she'd met along the way. One of the people she invited to her party was this young boy whose name was Sandy.

Sandy was almost eighteen and was more "experienced" than Sheila, if you know what I mean. As the party continued upstairs, Sheila and Sandy christened the party below in the basement.

Chapter 3

Sheila adored her parents. They gave her the world and opened doors that would've been otherwise closed. Prior to her sixteenth party, Sheila was a respectful, caring daughter. After her experience Sheila became very flippant and rebellious.

Lillie was very acute and immediately became bothered by Sheila's behavior. Lillie began to investigate her suspicious. Lillie was a typical mother-nosy. Nosiness and motherhood are synonymous.

After taking a snoop, Lillie blatantly asked Sheila if she was pregnant. Sheila replied with a "No, I have a tumor."
Lillie said, "Yeah right. A nine month tumor."

Sheila was definitely "in her feelings" by this time and decided to have an abortion.

Chapter 4

Sheila had her mind made up and "didn't want to change any shitty diapers." Sandy offered support and attempted to take some responsibility. Although he was only eighteen, he was willing to step up and do his part.

Lillie and Aaron pleaded with Sheila to not have an abortion. After alot of harassment and conviction, Sheila finally conceded. Deep down they knew that the brunt of raising this child would be on them but they could bear living with themselves if Sheila had an abortion.

They remained prayerful that Sheila would one day want to be a mother and love this child as she was loved.

The scuttlebutt of rustic town began to run rampant with the pregnancy of this teen. The Barbers were always good respectable people, how could Sheila's behavior have gotten past them?

The gossip finally subsided on November 9, 1975 when the baby was born.

Chapter 5

Sheila went through the formalities of choosing a name for the baby. Sandy was not around for the delivery but came shortly thereafter. He wanted his name on the birth certificate but Sheila's parents did not allow it.

Sheila fancied the name Heather Michelle. Sandy wanted the baby named after him. After several debates the name April Leigh was decided upon.

Motherhood was annoying and mundane to Sheila. Sheila was just as feral as ever and eventually stopped pretending to remotely care about this life that she had created. Because of that, the Barbers legally adopted April at age three in 1978 and began the process of parenting once more.

The Barbers were sexagenarians who should've planning their "Golden Years" not raising their grandchild

Chapter 6

At age nineteen, Sheila marries a man who is forty-two years old. What in the world could she have been thinking? Where in the world would they have even met? Sheila swore that she was in love when she married "Buddy." Lillie swore that Sheila married for spite and to get out of the house. Sheila was living lavish loca and baby April was forgotten.

Buddy had a daughter around five years old named Jeannie. What in the hell made Buddy think that Sheila would make a good stepmother when she had cast her own seed away?

The newlyweds settled into a two bedroom trailer in the country. The Barbers visited them at least once a week. Sheila and her husband didn't live far and I'm sure they hoped that Sheila would want to bond with April.

What normal child visits her mother and her new family? Growing up with the feeling and knowledge of being unwanted can form biased opinions of love, family, and life in general. If

April's opinions of love are fucked up, it wouldn't entirely be her fault.

Marriage did not slow Sheila's fast-lane life down one bit. She attended college but did not complete her Degree. She did manage to obtain a CNA license. Oddly enough Sheila liked caring for older people.

She worked various jobs, mostly in the food industry. She would occasionally attempt factory work but was always relieved of her duties due to her asthma.

Buddy was the only one working in this new union. The bills began to pile up and life became overwhelming. Something needed to be done and quick.

Chapter 7

By the age of twenty-one, you should be exonerated from your childish ways. Some have a smooth transition and then there was Sheila. She began a life of crime and drugs. She shoplifted and forged signatures to obtain other peoples' hard-earned money.

April was with Sheila in the grocery store and stole a stack of Polaroid camera film. You didn't need a receipt, so it was an easy hustle. April inadvertently became Sheila's co-conspirator at an early age.

The fact that Sheila had began to do drugs could've been kept a secret if April hadn't found a needle while playing in Sheila and Buddy's car. Sheila attempted to lie about the needle saying that it belonged to Buddy's diabetic sister but even at age eight, April was not duped.

It wasn't long before the pieces of the puzzle began to fit. Sheila was busted for shoplifting which brought her life to an abrupt halt. Sheila was sentenced to prison leaving her parents, new blended family, and Oh Yeah, April behind.

April desperately wanted to be a part of Sheila's life. It is unfortunate that Sheila did not want to be a part of April's. Sheila completed her sentence with the support of Buddy and her parents. Where was April's support system?

Chapter 8

Sue was an accomplice of Sheila's. She was some runabout homegirl that Sheila befriended along the way. Sue fell down on her luck and moved in with Sheila, Buddy, and Jeannie.

Buddy endured more than most would have. Either he was truly in love or the sex was off-the-chain. Once again no one in the household is working except Buddy. Sue was an ambitionless drug addict who was almost responsible for Sheila ODing once. Where in the world did Sheila find these people?

The bills had gotten so behind that Sheila and the rest were evicted. The Barbers came to the rescue by allowing the evictees to crash with them at the Barbers own a 3-bedroom ranch style house until they got on their feet. It was perfect for the three of them but very cramped for seven.

It doesn't make any sense why no one sent Sue packing. She crashed on a cot in April's room. The other three shared an unoccupied bedroom.

By all the mess that Sue made, you wouldn't know that she was an adult if you didn't see her. Sheila may've physically lived back at home but she was rarely present. She found sporadic employment which Aaron usually drove her to.

The cramped living quarters took a toll on April, more so than the others. Jeannie and April had an altercation. That was the final straw and the intruders found a new place of residence. Not a moment too soon.

Chapter 9

You'd think that Sheila would've tamed her wicked ways by now but no such luck. Sheila still partied like a teenager and continued her life of crime.

Sheila stayed out for days and weeks on end and returned as if nothing happened. What in the world was so important that it drew her away from everyone who attempted to love her?

Sheila came in at 2 in the morning, belligerent and drunk. Buddy and Sheila got into a physical altercation and Buddy cut Sheila across the forehead with a knife. Buddy apologized and wanted to take Sheila to the emergency room but for once in her life Sheila was afraid of someone. Sheila called her parents who woke April and picked Sheila up where Sheila received twenty-two stitches as a reminder of her behavior.

Buddy attempted to rekindle their marriage but too many tears had been shed and too many lives altered. Sheila was in the same emotional position that April was in—not knowing who to trust.

Chapter 10

After six years in a shattered marriage, Sheila divorces and moves back in with her parents. Along with the divorce comes another prison bid for Sheila. Hearing the recording "You have a collect call from (say your name)" gets old really quickly. The Barbers have been focusing on April and instilling positive values that would follow her in the future instead they were still babysitting Sheila and her antics.

Prison has a lot of rules regarding the type of clothing the inmates can have. Sheila's parents took care of those special details as usual. The three of them even visited Sheila on occasion. They made the three hour trek to see Sheila and to make sure once again that she was okay.

At times it seemed as though Sheila was still the child. There's usually one that requires move attention than the other and Sheila was definitely that child.

Chapter 11

Free again in the fast lane of life. With a new sense of freedom comes new friends for Sheila. The newest friend is a German woman named Michelle. She's pale in complexion and shaves off her eyebrows. The strangest part is that she draws them back on entirely too high on her forehead.

There's also a new boyfriend who's Nigerian. He and Sheila move into a roach-infested apartment. I know that it's customary for Africans to sit on the floor and eat foo foo but the thought of it nauseates me. Africans can be very controlling and with Sheila's untamed ways, this relationship was very short-lived.

Directly behind the unnamed African was Alan. He is violent and extremely jealous. He was also very shrewd and "played" April for information. Alan inquired about Sheila's whereabouts and discovered that she was at the beach with a platonic friend named Mickey. April had no idea that the information divulged should've been kept a secret nor that it would've landed Sheila several bruised.

Chapter 12

Sheila worked on her craft of thievery. She could steal the stink off shit, the moo from a cow, and the tears of a clown. You could always tell when she was going out to boost. She carried a black or pink pocketbook. That was a sure sign that some store's inventory was about to be short.

April was aware of Sheila's "job" but never approved of it. Sheila would often bring April gifts attempting to buy her love and approval. April accepted the gifts but most were short-lived because Sheila would take them back to exchange for drugs. She always promised to bring something else in its place.

The only thing that April wanted Sheila to bring was herself. All April wanted was her mother.

Chapter 13

Sheila's on her own in an apartment. She actually obtained it by herself through subsidized housing. The neighborhood was not ideal but Sheila didn't seem to mind.

There was always drama in the "projects." That's slang for the hood. Someone was always stealing, had a radio blaring, or being some place that she shouldn't. Illegal activities were always plentiful there.

Once when April came over she found some boy hiding in Sheila's closet. Who knows why he was there. April learned at an early age to have a "don't ask, don't tell" policy.

Chapter 14

There were always countless trips on places to take Sheila. She was technically free from prison but had alot of community service to do. This free labor had been in lieu of a lesser sentence to serve.

Sheila would often put on a facade between she and April when they were in public. There were brief intervals when they actually did hang out. April would jump on Sheila's back for the classic "piggy back" ride and even gave her the nickname of "Beefy" because of Sheila's ample backside.

Things were far from Kosher between the two because April was numb to Sheila's lies and shenanigans. April was almost a teenager and had given up on the possibility of ever having a mother.

Chapter 15

When Sheila lived at home, she half-assed acted as she should. She respects her parents' rules of not coming in all hours of the night, or so they think. What she should've adhered to was a dress code. Sheila was plus-size, boobs and butt and often did not wear the appropriate clothing size.

Lounging around the house is one thing but going in public in a tube top and biker shorts should've been against the law. Sheila rarely wore age appropriate clothes which often embarrassed April and should've embarrassed Sheila herself.

One of Sheila's friends who drove a cab came by to give her a ride. Aaron disapproved of Sheila's attire and spoke up about it. Sheila exuded her defiance and eventually got in the cab but not before Aaron chased her with one of April's toy baseball bats.

Chapter 16

April covered up for Sheila alot when she crashed at home. The roles of mother/daughter seemed to have been switched at an early age. As you could've probably guessed, Sheila had no household skills. The ironing, cooking, and cleaning that was supposed to be Sheila's task was completed by April. April who was hip to the game, made Sheila pay her for her services.

On the nights that Sheila was extremely late, she'd tap on April's window so that Lillie and Aaron weren't disturbed. April let her in and ensured that she did not make a mess.

Once in one of Sheila's drunken stupors, April rebraided her hair. It had fresh braids which would've easily been noticed if they had been in disarray. None of this was fair to April.

Despite this disturbing home life April was a honor roll student and was in a lot of public events such as spelling bees and speech contests. One only one occasion did Sheila ever make an appearance. If April had not had her grandparents she would've been truly alone.

On another of Sheila's benders, she opened a can of cold soup and put it in a bowl on the nightstand. In Sheila's drug induced mind she was reaching for the bowl. In reality she was diving into the air in slow motion that landed her in the floor.

Sheila paid April for her silence once again. This became a very lucrative relationship for April. Too bad that April wasn't paid for the lies that Sheila dished. She would've been a billionaire by high school.

Chapter 17

By the time April was a teenager she was already experienced. Apparently it must be hereditary. But the Barbers thought that surely Sheila would be responsible enough to stay with April when they were away. This couldn't have been farther from the truth.

Sheila stayed glued to the phone from sun up to sun down. Sheila was always planning her next moves. While she was doing that, April made moves of her own. I would say that she "snuck" boys in but there was no need to sneak. The boys would simply give Sheila a nod or a "Hey Ma" and keep it moving.

That was one of the few times that April and Sheila were on the same accord.

Chapter 18

Sheila always had a fetish for older men. Perhaps they reminded her of Aaron. Maybe she felt safer with a father figure. Who knows? She needed someone to watch over her and her parents would not live forever. And I seriously doubt that April would've signed up for that task.

The next victim on Sheila's list was Bobby. He seemed a little more stable than the others. He worked two jobs and attended school part-time. Bobby was different than the guys Sheila normally dated. He did not do drugs and only had the occasional beer. Where in the world could they have met? Bobby was somewhat settled. Could Shelia be growing up a little?

Bobby lavished Sheila with anything she wanted which lasted about two years. Stability seemed to bore Sheila and before long, she was back to her old ways.

Sheila had stooped to a new low when she withdrew money from April's saving account. April had learned how to save money at an early age. She had a summer job and saved her money for the future.

Sheila forged Lillie's name that accompanied April's name on the account. April was so livid that she became physical with Sheila. Sheila of course swore to repay April but she knew that was a lie. If lying was a sport, Sheila was surely a gold medalist.

When April was young and naive all she wanted was Sheila's love and acknowledgment. As a teenager, she just wanted to be left alone and had given up on the belief that Sheila would ever change.

Chapter 19

Sheila was raised in the church. Both Aaron and Lillie were active members. April was forced to go to church also but she never felt as though she "fit." She found it to be judgmental and not what she wanted to pattern her life by.

April shed many tears at church because of Sheila's lies. Sheila promised to come to church so April would stare at the wooden doors hoping that when they opened Sheila would appear. What kind of mother would lie about church?

This formed alot of April's opinions and beliefs about the existence of God and religion. Where was He when April needed Him most?

Chapter 20

When Bobby had had enough it truly showed. Their breakup exposed a side of Sheila that no one had ever seen. Until Bobby, everyone in Sheila life seemed replaceable. The breakup turned Sheila into a stalker. She popped up at his place of work, sent flowers, and coerced April to talk to him in hopes to reconcile.

The two never rekindled and if Sheila had known that Bobby had made advances towards April she probably wouldn't have wanted to. The relationship was dead and there was no need in adding fuel to the fire. This nugget of information remained a secret forever.

Chapter 21

The revolving door of the Barbers' home was opened once again to Sheila. She followed the usual routine of finding employment only to quit in the near future. As long as she made an effort, the mooching off of her parents was minimal.

April began to gain a little freedom and was allowed to go to the movies with Sheila. Being chaperoned by Sheila was the equivalent of running with a pack of wolves.

April met a man twice her age at her summer job who became her boyfriend. Sheila helped them sneak around for a small fee. April's boyfriend drove Sheila to pick April up from school and in turn they would drop Sheila off at various stores to "boost."

April and her boyfriend gave Sheila a little money for her troubles. Bribery keeps this family together.

Chapter 22

There had been so much focus on Sheila that no one had bothered to guide April in the direction in which she needed to go. The Barbers were strict on April, because they did not want history to repeat itself. Because of this, the opposite occurred.

April was arrested and charged with the death of her grandparents and her boyfriend was charged with conspiracy. You'd think that she'd at least have the support of Sheila but you'd have guessed wrong. In fact, Sheila skipped town without a trace. She was gone for so long that the funeral had to be delayed.

As a matter of fact, Sheila hated April. April had removed her safety net and had no one to rely on but herself. They were finally on the same level.

Chapter 23

April had been incarcerated roughly two years when Sheila returned. There was still nothing bittersweet about their relationship. Sheila was still Dr. Jekyll and Ms. Hyde in front of people and the real her behind closed doors.

Sheila befriended April's friends because she noticed that April managed to have what she needed despite being alone. April reluctantly supplied Sheila with the basics while feeding her with a long-handle spoon.

April desperately wanted to move forward. She was dealing with her issues but Sheila refused to let go of the past which triggered April and caused verbal retaliation. The ones outside of April's circle would make snide comments like "I Can't Believe You Talk To Your Mother Like That!" April would fire back with a quick, "Mind Your Damn Business!"

April's friends were older than her and had been in the system longer than her. They recognized Sheila's game. They assisted in diffusing situations between April and outsiders. They kept meddlesome people in their place.

The months that Sheila was in prison seemed like eons. Just when April was able to move forward a step, Sheila would bring up painful memories that threw her two steps back.

Sheila attempted to leave on a better note than she came promising to write, visit, send money and find a lawyer to help April obtain freedom. April heard these words but knew deep down they were false.

Chapter 24

The years passed like the silence of Sheila's promises within them. Sheila's profession brought her back to prison when April was around twenty. Damn, why couldn't she just stay away?

The more Sheila was around the worse April's life was. Incarceration was mentally taxing in itself without the added stress of Sheila's presence. The arguments became frequent and damn near volatile at times between the two. Sheila blamed April for removing her security blanket. Never once was Sheila accountable for her own fuck ups.

April was without the people that raised her also. She had been without parents basically her entire life but that seemed to be cast aside. She had been alone to make decisions that needed a second opinion and no one but the penal system was around to help April.

Fortunately before things exploded, Sheila transferred to another prison. April was grateful for the separation and hopeful that this would be their last visit together.

April received an unexpected letter from Sheila about two weeks after her departure. The contents consisted of the usual lies and snide remarks until the closing which read, "Have a happy life, sentence that is." What kind of person much less a mother could be so cruel? It was not April that was the sadistic monster, it was Sheila. With a mother like hers, who needs enemies.

Chapter 25

April is serving a life sentence so the only way that someone new enters her life is if they go to her. Instead of meeting someone new, Sheila's familiar face reappeared in 1995. Same old song and dance. This shit is really old. And would you believe that Sheila still has the gall to expect April to supply her needs? April's totally desensitized to Sheila and her BS. She doesn't care one way or the other.

Prison provides structure. Contrary to belief, you cannot roam around, watch TV, and eating bon-bons all day. You must work and if you want to better yourself you will educate yourself. This is what April did. She had little free time which was a blessing since Sheila was once again in prison.

April was able to avoid Sheila and any potential major catastrophes.

Chapter 26

A couple of years expired before April heard from Sheila. Sheila had met some man and lived in Virginia. At least if she went to prison it wouldn't be in North Carolina. As luck would have, that's exactly what happened.

She had no employment or vehicle. She said that she'd lost weight because she had to walk everywhere she went. Her boyfriend sounded like the same losers that she always dated but Sheila was sober. She had given up drugs and said that she only drank on occasion. Was her occasions like the song, "Day and Night?"

Sheila began the myriad of promises i.e. helping financially, writing, etc. April cut her short and told her that if she was truly sincere she'd put actions behind her words.

At the age of twenty-five, April had developed issues of her own. She was diagnosed with Multiple Sclerosis (MS) and was dealing with that. She was a CNA and was very familiar with the disease and its unpredictability.

For once Sheila sounded as if she genuinely cared but it was too little, too late. She never cared before, so why bother now?

Chapter 27

Sheila called the social worker sporadically to check on April. The social worker who'd become a mother liaison allowed them to talk via phone. The same worker was there when Sheila began her first prison sentence and knew her well.

The damage between April and Sheila was irreparable. April wanted to more forward and the past behind her. The phone calls and rare letters became infrequent which was just fine with April.

Chapter 28

The social worker was a saint. She was one of the sweetest women that you'd ever meet. Another almost two years passed without a peep from Sheila. Had April finally gotten her wish? The social worker would ask April if she'd heard from Sheila. She'd always shrug with a "No."

The social worker's gut feeling must've sensed that something was up because she began to constantly ask April of the whereabouts of Sheila. It was almost annoying.

Chapter 29

On a warm June day in 2003, April was summoned to the social worker's office. This wasn't uncommon but as she neared the office an eerie feeling crept upon her.

When she arrived she looked as though she'd seen a ghost. Visitation was only on the weekends, so civilians were not allowed on the grounds at any other time. Suzette, who was a long time family friend was in the social worker's cramped office.

Silence filled the room as Suzette handed me a newspaper article that read about a nameless woman being killed by a taxi. The next of kin had not been notified so the name had not been released.

After calls were made it was confirmed that the victim was in fact Sheila who had returned to North Carolina. Sheila had a blood alcohol level of .34, four hours after impact. Hell, that was one of her light days.

The accident was ruled as just that—an accident. April retained a wrongful death attorney but the driver was not found at fault. The situation never settled well with April. Sheila was uninsured and basically homeless but she was if only by name, April's mother.

Chapter 30

At age twenty-seven, April took the money that she had been saving and buried Sheila. There was a funeral home that assisted with inmates and paupers. They were very nice in assisting April with the arrangements.

April attended a private viewing, all be it shackled due to her incarceration she was finally able to give Sheila a resting place. Sheila no longer has to run wild, planning her next get-rich-quick-scheme.

My Mother

Fast life, drugs, and prison . . .
Beefy died at the hands of some else.
Out of all the things she'd done . . .
I thought that she would've done it to herself.
I have my regrets because I should've
been a better daughter.
My supporters remind me to not be
so hard on myself.
She could've been a better mother.
Nevertheless she's gone and never to returned . . .
This has been my lesson learned.
I'll miss you Beefty.

RIP

www.ingramcontent.com/pod-product-compliance
Lightning Source LLC
Chambersburg PA
CBHW052107110526
44591CB00013B/2380